the **complete** *series*

Soups

WILEY

John Wiley & Sons, Inc.

For general information on our other products and services or for technical support, please contact our Customer Care Department within the United States at (877) 762-2974, outside the United States at (317) 572-3993 or fax (317) 572-4002.

Wiley also publishes its books in a variety of electronic formats. Some content that appears in print may not be available in electronic books. For more information about Wiley products, visit our web site at www.wiley.com.

Library of Congress Cataloging-in-Publication Data is available upon request.

ISBN 978-1-118-17052-6

Printed in the United States of America

10 9 8 7 6 5 4 3 2 1

Contents

Introduction

Soup is one of the most basic foods. Its history stretches far into the past when soup was simply water simmered with whatever basic ingredients were available for flavor. Soup then was never about quality ingredients and complex flavors. Rather, it was simply about survival. Yet soup was still a meal shared between family members and acquaintances.

Thick hearty soups are served in the cold months to nourish and satisfy hungry children and to give energy to people at the end of a hectic day.

Cold refreshing soups are served in hot weather and humid climates to invigorate and enliven after an exhausting day.

Throughout the Western world soups are served as a teaser to the coming meal, while in China soup is served after a meal as an invigorating finale. In many European countries soup is served between courses to refresh the palate.

In fact, soup is served more often and in many more flavor combinations throughout the world than any other meal.

Soups have changed in many ways over the years, with modern cooking methods and ingredients taking over from traditional methods and ingredients.

What would Great Grandpa have said if Great Grandma had served him up a soup of onions cooked in white wine and brandy? The very idea! Soups made from rock melon and peaches. Soups with Japanese liqueur in them. Soups served chilled!

Ah yes times have changed.

It could be argued that the level of a nation's culinary sophistication can be seen in the soups it serves. There's nothing wrong with good old traditionals like beef shin or calf's foot, however we tend now to use more modern ingredients.

The modern cook prefers to stay away from the predictable and concentrate on a selection of recipes that use imaginative ingredients in imaginative ways. In the recipe selection offered in these chapters we include, with the traditional, some delightful variations.

When planning your dinner party, choose your soup carefully. A dinner of several courses should be preceded by a light clear soup, preferably a consommé. Thick soups, on the other hand, should be regarded as part of the main meal. And, of course, fruit soups may be served before or after the meal.

Soups are time-honored comfort foods, with well-rounded flavors and soothing, sustained warmth. Prepared more often in a single pot, they can incorporate all kinds of ingredients in combinations that are as nutritious as they are delicious.

Be lost in a sense of well-being as the contents of your cooking pot boil and bubble and the tendrils of steam and aroma curl up, permeating the surroundings and inducing a real warmth and homely feeling. What dreary winter afternoon is not brightened by the companionable murmur of a simmering soup on the stove?

A soup can be thick or thin, it can range from a clear, light broth to a hearty chowder almost thick enough to eat with a knife and fork. It has been noted that several centuries ago soup was served over 5 courses as a total meal. This has not been repeated in these modern times to our knowledge.

At the turn of the century it was normal to have soup always be served as part of the evening meal. These days however, we are not as regimented and soup can be served at any time of the night or day and in almost any position on the menu – from snack to main course, from entrée to dessert. Or indeed, soups can and sometimes do constitute an entire meal.

So you will see in these recipes that a soup can be served as a first course, a main course, or even – when made with fruit – a dessert. It can also be a between-meal snack, to satisfy those cheeky customers just home from school or work.

Our selected recipes offer soups of all types for all occasions and are built upon one of the basic stock recipes that appear in this introduction. Most are simple to prepare and in most situations require a minimum investment in time.

Of course, we offer slow-cooked soups as well as some real fast heat and serve varieties, a selection of recipes to suit all appetites and tastes.

Techniques

While soup is very easy to make and delightfully satisfying to eat, there is no doubt that a few tricks of the trade and some handy hints will give you superior results, even if you have never made a pot of soup before.

Cookware

While quality cookware is always a joy to use, remember that soups are centuries old and most of our ancestors didn't have the pleasure of shiny new cookware and elegant stovetops. Just use whatever large saucepans or stockpots you have. If you find you need a new saucepan, purchase a high-quality pot with a strong enamel or non-stick surface, or a stainless steel pot that has an insulated base. Cast iron works well too.

Ingredients

We all want to use the best, freshest ingredients when we prepare foods for our family or friends, and there is no doubt that quality ingredients contribute towards a more delicious and healthy end result. Meat, fish, poultry, spices and herbs should always be in peak condition for the best soups. Vegetables, however, can be a little wilted or past their prime. When you are about to make a soup or stock, clean out your vegetable crisper and see what has been left behind. Of course, common-sense should prevail, so don't use any vegetables that smell unpleasant or are obviously mouldy.

Most soups freeze well. When freezing any liquid, leave a 5mm space between the soup and the lid of the container, as liquid expands during freezing.

Home-made stocks – foundations of flavor

The basis of a quality soup is a quality stock – it's as simple as that! In years past, a good soup always began with hours of simmering simple vegetables and, perhaps, some meat bones to create a rich broth.

These days, however, if you prefer to bypass this step, there are several prepared stocks available from your local supermarket. They can be found in liquid form, as a paste or as a powder.

Generally speaking, it is much easier to purchase liquid stocks as they have a true flavor and are literally ready to use. Pastes are a good option too because they are concentrated, which allows you to add as much water as necessary to dilute the flavor according to your tastes.

In our opinion, most stock powders should be avoided if the liquid or paste stocks are available. These powders are often heavily salted and therefore offer a salty rather than 'true to taste' flavor. The ratio of powder to water can be difficult to master and some brands contain artificial flavors and colors.

By far the most rewarding and delicious stock is the one you make yourself. Contrary to popular belief, stocks are not difficult to make and, although they do need to simmer for quite some time, their preparation time is minimal.

The following recipes will guide you through the basics of making a good stock – regardless of which type of stock you wish to make, you can follow one of these basic methods. If you have any vegetables in your refrigerator that are looking a little wilted and sad, throw these into the stockpot too as they will add extra flavor and color.

Oh, and one other thing – remember that stocks freeze extremely well for extended periods of time, so don't be afraid to make a pot of stock when you have large amounts of vegetables, roasted meat bones or turkey frames (from the Christmas bird) on hand. Make the stock and pop it in the freezer for your future risotto or soup.

Making good stock is a very simple procedure. The ingredients are simmered in a pot – when strained and degreased the cooking liquid becomes a savoury extract to serve on its own, store for later use, or use in preparing another dish. Recipes for the five basic stocks follow on the next pages. Stock comes from humble beginnings – inexpensive cuts of meat and bones, fish bones and heads, or chicken wings and backs.

Attention to detail will reward you with a rich and tasty stock. All large fat deposits should be removed beforehand, but large bones will give you treasured gelatine, if cracked first, and provide body to your stock.

During cooking, remove scum that occasionally collects on top of the liquid. Scum consist of protein particles released by meat and bones, these float to the surface, where they gather in a foam. As nutritious as it is, the foam must be removed lest it cloud the stock. Skim off the foam as it forms at the start of cooking, skim thereafter only as the recipe directs.

After its initial rapid cooking, stock must not be allowed to return to rapid boil as the turbulence will muddy the liquid. As a final cleansing, the stock should be strained through a fine sieve or a colander lined with muslin.

Storage

To prepare stock for storage, divide it among containers surrounded with iced water. Wait until the stock has cooled to cover the containers, otherwise it may sour. Refrigerated in covered containers, any of these stocks will keep up to three days. The fat on top of the stock will form a temporary seal, helping to keep it fresh – you need not degrease the stock until shortly before you are ready to use it.

To prolong the life of refrigerated stock, first remove and discard the congealed fat, then boil the stock for five minutes – either freeze the stock or boil it again every three days. As always, cool it quickly and uncovered before storing it once more.

Fish and vegetable stock may be frozen for two months. Stock destined for the freezer must first be degreased, as frozen fat can turn rancid.

One Final Note

You will notice that the recipes in this book usually serve 4–8 or more people. This is because soup generally keeps very well and is often even better on the second or third day. Therefore, one recipe can offer you sustenance and an easy nutritional choice for several meals. If you prefer not to make such a large serve, or if you are cooking for only one or two people, most of these recipes can be halved successfully.

Rich Vegetable Stock

Suggested Ingredients
2 tablespoons olive oil
1 turnip or parsnip
5 cloves garlic
3 stalks celery
3 large carrots
10 mushrooms
3 large onions
4 tomatoes
2 leeks, well washed
2 parsnips
10 sprigs parsley
1 teaspoon peppercorns
4 bay leaves

1 Wash all the vegetables and chop roughly.

2 Heat the olive oil in a large stockpot and sauté all the vegetables for 20 minutes until they begin to develop a golden color on the surface.

3 Add the parsley, peppercorns, bay leaves and water to cover (about 4 quarts/liters) and bring to a boil. Simmer for 3 hours, skimming the surface to remove any scum that accumulates.

4 Add salt if desired, then simmer for an additional few minutes if you would like a more intense flavor. Allow to cool then strain, pressing on the solids. Use within three days or freeze for up to 12 months.

These are some suggested vegetables for a rich stock, but you can use whatever you have on hand. Even vegetables that are past their prime work just fine—Brussels sprouts, bell peppers, even corn.

Makes 8 cups • Preparation 25 minutes • Cooking 2 hours

Chicken Stock

Suggested Ingredients
2 carrots
4 stalks celery
3 onions
1 leek, chopped
8 sprigs parsley, chopped
2kg/4 lb chicken frames or wings
1 teaspoon peppercorns

1 Wash all the vegetables and chop roughly.
2 Place all ingredients in a large stockpot. Add water to generously cover the ingredients (about 4 quarts/liters). Bring to a boil then simmer for 2–3 hours, skimming the scum off the surface as it rises to the top.
3 Add salt if desired, then strain the stock through a sieve lined with cheesecloth.
4 Place in a large saucepan and chill until the fat solidifies on the surface. Remove the fat and use or freeze.

Makes 10 cups • Preparation 20 minutes • Cooking 3 hours

Fish Stock

Suggested Ingredients
500g/1 lb fish bones, heads and trimmings, washed
2 carrots, chopped
4 stalks celery, chopped
3 onions, roughly chopped
8 sprigs parsley, chopped
6 white peppercorns
good pinch of ground nutmeg
1 teaspoon salt

1 Place the fish pieces and 4 cups water into a saucepan and bring to a boil.
2 Skim off any discolored froth from the top. Add remaining ingredients and simmer gently, uncovered, for an additional 30 minutes. If cooked too long the stock becomes bitter.
3 Strain and discard the bones and vegetables. Use the stock within two days or freeze it in a sealed container.

Makes 4 cups • Preparation 30 minutes • Cooking 40 minutes

Shrimp Stock

Suggested Ingredients
1kg/2 lb shrimp shells and heads
2 carrots
4 stalks celery
3 onions
1 leek
8 sprigs parsley, chopped
1 teaspoon peppercorns

1 Thoroughly wash shells and heads.
2 Wash all the vegetables and chop roughly. Place in a large stockpot with the shrimp shells, heads, parsley and peppercorns. Cover with 4 quarts/ liters cold water and bring to a boil. Reduce heat to simmer and cook for 1–2 hours, skimming the skum off the surface as it forms.
3 Add salt to taste, then strain through a sieve lined with cheesecloth.
4 Place in a large saucepan and chill until the fat solidifies on the surface. Remove the fat and use or freeze the stock.

Makes 4 cups • Preparation 35 minutes • Cooking 2 hours

Veal Stock

Suggested Ingredients
1kg/2 lb veal breast or shin, cut into 3 in/75mm pieces
2kg/4 lb veal bones, cracked (preferably knuckles)
2 carrots
4 stalks celery
3 onions
4 sprigs fresh thyme, leaves removed and stalks discarded
3 unpeeled cloves garlic, crushed
8 black peppercorns
1 bay leaf

1 Rinse veal bones with water.
2 Wash all the vegetables and chop roughly. Place in a large stockpot with the veal bones, meat and remaining ingredients.
3 Wash all the vegetables and slice or chop roughly. Then place in a large stockpot with the veal bones and meat and all remaining ingredients.
4 Cover with cold water (about 4 quarts/liters), bring to a boil and simmer for 2–3 hours, skimming the scum off the surface as it rises to the top.
5 Add salt if desired, then strain through a sieve lined with cheesecloth.
6 Place in a large saucepan and chill until the fat solidifies on the surface. Remove the fat and use or freeze the stock.

Makes 10 cups • Preparation 30 minutes • Cooking 4 hours

Beef Stock

Suggested Ingredients
1kg/2 lb beef, cut into 3 in/75mm pieces
2kg/4 lb beef bones, cracked
2 carrots, chopped
4 stalks celery, chopped
3 onions, chopped
3 unpeeled cloves garlic, crushed
8 black peppercorns
3 cloves
4 sprigs fresh thyme, leaves removed and stalks discarded
1 bay leaf

1 Preheat oven to 220°C, place meat, bones, carrots, celery and onions in a large roasting pan and roast for about 1 hour, until well browned.
2 Transfer the contents of the roasting pan to a large saucepan. Pour 2 cups of water into the roasting pan and, with a spatula, scrape up all the brown bits from the bottom and sides of the pan. Pour this liquid into the large saucepan.
3 Add the garlic, peppercorns and cloves. Pour in enough water to cover the contents of the saucepan by about 3 in/75mm. Bring to a boil, then reduce heat to a simmer and skim off any impurities from the surface. Add the thyme and bay leaf, then simmer the stock for about 4 hours, skimming occasionally.
4 When cooked, strain the stock, allow to cool and refrigerate until fat solidifies on the surface. Remove the fat and use or freeze the stock.

Makes 10 cups • Preparation 40 minutes • Cooking 5 hours

Beef

Vegetable Beef Soup

2kg/4 lb beef shanks
2 tablespoons olive oil
1 teaspoon salt
1 small onion, chopped
450g/16 oz canned diced tomatoes
6 sprigs parsley
5 carrots, sliced
100g/3½ oz green beans, cut diagonally
1 medium potato, diced
1 stalk celery, chopped
¼ cup barley

1 In a heavy-based frying pan, brown the meat in the olive oil. Pour off excess fat and oil.
2 Cover with 8 cups cold water and bring to a boil. Add salt and onion, simmer for 2 hours.
3 Add vegetables and barley. Simmer for about 1 hour longer. Remove meat from bone, add back to soup and serve.

Serves 8 • Preparation 30 minutes • Cooking 3 hours 15 minutes

Beef Barley Soup

⅓ cup wholewheat flour
1 teaspoon salt
500g/1 lb lean stewing beef
2 tablespoons olive oil
1 medium onion, chopped
4 large cloves garlic, minced
½ medium carrot, grated
1 stalk celery, chopped
1 large tomato, diced
1 cup barley
5 cups chicken stock
¼ cup basil, chopped
1 bay leaf
salt and freshly ground black pepper

1 In a plastic bag, combine flour, salt and meat. Shake vigorously.

2 In a large saucepan, pour in the oil and quickly brown the meat over medium heat. Add onions and garlic and cook until soft, about 3–4 minutes. Add the carrot, celery and tomato and continue cooking for about 5 minutes.

3 Add barley, stock and basil and bring to a boil. Wrap the bay leaf in cheesecloth and add to the pot. Lower heat and allow to simmer until the barley is soft, about 20–25 minutes.

4 Season to taste with the salt and pepper. Remove bay leaf before serving.

Serves 8 • Preparation 20 minutes • Cooking 30 minutes

Meatball Soup

500g/1 lb ground beef
1 medium onion, finely chopped
¼ cup parsley, chopped
¼ cup medium-grain rice
2 eggs
salt and freshly ground black pepper
⅓ cup cornstarch
4 cups beef stock
50g/3½ tablespoons butter
⅓ cup lemon juice

1 Combine the mince, onion, parsley, rice and 1 egg in a bowl, and mix well with your hands. Season well with salt and pepper. Using one tablespoon of mixture for each meatball, shape mixture into balls. Roll in cornstarch, shaking off any excess.

2 Bring the stock and the butter to a boil, then reduce the heat and place the meatballs in the stock. Cover and simmer for 45 minutes. Allow to cool slightly.

3 Whisk the remaining egg and lemon juice together in a bowl, then add ½ cup of warm stock. Pour this mixture back into the saucepan and heat very gently. Season with salt and pepper before serving.

Serves 4 • Preparation 20 minutes • Cooking 1 hour 10 minutes

Cabbage Soup

30g/2 tablespoons butter
250g/9 oz beef, diced
125g/4½ oz chopped bacon
300g/10 oz cabbage, finely shredded
2 large tomatoes, peeled and diced
2 onions, diced
1 bay leaf
salt and freshly ground black pepper
4 cups beef stock
⅓ cup sour cream
40g/1.4 oz Parmesan cheese, grated

1 Melt butter in a large saucepan and sauté beef and bacon over a medium heat until browned.
2 Add half the cabbage and all the remaining ingredients except sour cream and Parmesan. Cover, bring to a boil, and simmer for 1½ hours. Add remaining cabbage and cook for 10–15 minutes or until tender. Stir in cream, sprinkle with Parmesan cheese and serve.

Serves 6 • Preparation 15 minutes • Cooking 2 hours

Hearty Beef Soup

100g/3½ oz chickpeas
100g/3½ oz dried split peas
3 tablespoons butter
3 tablespoons mild curry powder
3 tablespoons garam masala
3 tablespoons fresh minced ginger
3 cloves garlic, minced
4 large onions, diced
2 leeks, well washed and chopped

400g/14 oz ground beef
3 medium carrots, grated
2 stalks celery, finely sliced
1 small cauliflower, divided into florets
1 bunch fresh cilantro, chopped
8 cups chicken or beef stock
4 tablespoons yogurt
salt and pepper to taste

1 Place the chickpeas and split peas in a large bowl of water and soak for 30 minutes. Drain. Heat the butter in a large saucepan and add the curry powder, garam masala, ginger and garlic and sauté until the spices are fragrant, about 3 minutes. Add the onions and leeks and cook over a medium-high heat until the onions have softened and are beginning to turn golden, about 6 minutes.

2 Add the minced beef and cook in the spice and onion mixture, making sure that the meat is thoroughly cooked and fragrant before continuing.

3 Add the carrots, celery, cauliflower, half the chopped fresh cilantro, the stock and the chickpea mixture and bring to a boil. Simmer the soup for 1½ hours or until the chickpeas are tender, stirring often.

4 When almost ready to serve, stir through the yogurt and add salt and pepper to taste. Garnish with the remaining chopped fresh cilantro and serve.

Serves 8–10 • Preparation 30 minutes plus 10 minutes soaking • Cooking 2 hours

Chicken

Chicken Vegetable Soup with Cheese Sticks

2 boneless, skinless chicken breasts
4 cups chicken stock
1 tablespoon canola oil
2 leeks, washed and thinly sliced
2 carrots, diced
2 stalks celery, diced
3 cloves garlic, crushed
6 cups spinach, arugula or escarole
3 tablespoons basil pesto
freshly cracked black pepper

Cheese Sticks
1 sheet puff pastry, thawed
40g/1.4 oz Cheddar cheese, finely grated

1 Put the chicken in a pot, add just enough chicken stock to cover it and poach gently for about 10 minutes or until just cooked. Set aside to cool.

2 Heat the oil in a large pot, add the leeks and cook gently for about 2 minutes until soft. Add the carrot, celery and garlic, strain the chicken poaching stock through a fine sieve and add to the vegetables with the rest of the stock. Simmer for 10 minutes. Chop the greens finely, add them to the soup and cook for an additional 10 minutes.

3 Shred the chicken breasts and add them to the soup. Stir in the pesto and season with plenty of cracked black pepper.

Cheese Sticks

1 Preheat the oven to 425°F/220°C. Cut the puff pastry into 1 in/2cm strips and place on a baking sheet lined with parchment paper. Sprinkle with the cheese and bake for 20 minutes or until crisp and golden.

2 Serve the soup in wide bowls with cheese sticks.

Serves 6 • Preparation 30 minutes • Cooking 40 minutes

Chicken Corn Chowder

1kg/2 lb chicken
½ cup water chestnuts, drained
1 small onion, peeled and halved
2 slices bacon, cooked and crumbled
½ in/1cm piece green ginger, peeled
450g/16 oz canned corn, drained reserving liquid
6 green onions, sliced
2 teaspoons sesame oil
salt and freshly ground black pepper
3 tablespoons cornstarch
1 tablespoon sherry
2 teaspoons soy sauce
1 egg

1 Wash chicken and place into a large saucepan with 10 cups water. Bring to a boil and simmer approximately 40 minutes or until chicken is cooked. Remove chicken from pan, set aside to cool. Do not discard chicken stock. While chicken is cooking, prepare other ingredients.

2 Place water chestnuts, onion, bacon and ginger into food processor or blender bowl and process until finely chopped. Remove from bowl.

3 Purée corn niblets in food processor or blender.

4 Remove skin and bones from chicken. Place chicken into processor bowl and process until finely chopped.

5 Take 2 cups of chicken stock from pan and reserve for future use.

6 Add all prepared ingredients with reserved corn liquid to chicken stock.

7 Add green onions to saucepan with sesame oil, salt and pepper. Bring to boil. Mix cornstarch and ⅓ cup water to a smooth paste, add to soup and simmer, stirring, for 3 minutes. Add sherry and soy sauce. Lightly beat egg with a fork, add to soup and stir for 1 minute. Serve.

Serves 12 • Preparation 40 minutes • Cooking 1 hour 30 minutes

Chicken and Leek Soup

1kg/2 lb chicken pieces
1 onion, chopped
1 carrot, peeled and chopped
pinch saffron
1 stalk celery, chopped
2 leeks, finely sliced
30g/2 tablespoons butter
salt
cayenne pepper
½ cup heavy cream

1 In a large pot, place the chicken, onion, carrot, saffron and celery. Cover the ingredients with water and boil for 1 hour.

2 Remove from the heat and strain off the stock. Reserve the chicken.

3 Sauté the leeks in the butter until soft, add the chicken stock and, heat through. Season with salt and cayenne pepper. Add cream as desired and serve.

Serves 6 • Preparation 10 minutes • Cooking 1 hour 15 minutes

Mulligatawny

30g/2 tablespoons butter
1 small onion, finely diced
½ in/1cm piece ginger, grated
1 tablespoon curry powder
1 tablespoon all-purpose flour
1 tablespoon desiccated coconut
4 cups chicken stock
1 bouquet garni
1 tablespoon tomato paste
1 tablespoon mango chutney
½ small banana, sliced
150g/5 oz cooked chicken breast, diced
juice of ½ lemon
salt and freshly ground black pepper

1 Melt butter in a saucepan over medium heat. Add onion, ginger and curry powder and cook until onion is tender. Add the flour and coconut and cook for an additional 2 minutes. Add the stock, bouquet garni and tomato paste. Bring to a boil and simmer over low heat for 45 minutes.

2 Add the chutney, banana, chicken, lemon juice and seasonings. Heat through, remove bouquet garni and serve sprinkled with boiled rice.

Serves 4 • Preparation 20 minutes • Cooking 1 hour

Matzo Ball Soup

Soup

2 tablespoons vegetable oil
3 large onions, chopped
3 large carrots, chopped
4 stalks celery, chopped
2kg/4 lb chicken bones, wings, scraps
4 bay leaves
6 sprigs parsley
300g/10 oz piece of beef top rib

Matzoh Balls

2 tablespoons vegetable oil
1 large onion, finely diced
4 large eggs
¼ small bunch chives, chopped
1–1½ cups matzoh meal
salt and freshly ground black pepper

1 First, make the soup. Heat the oil in a very large saucepan and add the onions, carrots and celery and sauté in the oil until golden, about 10 minutes. Add the chicken, bay leaves, parsley, beef and 4 quarts/liters of water and bring to a boil. Simmer for 5 hours, skimming the scum off the surface as it becomes visible. After 5 hours, taste the soup and season to taste. Chill the soup overnight.

2 The next day, skim the fat off the surface of the soup then reheat until just warm. Strain the soup into a clean saucepan, discarding the solids.

3 To make the matzoh balls, heat the vegetable oil in a frying pan and add the finely chopped onions. Sauté until the onions are deep golden brown. Remove the pan from the heat and add the eggs, chives, matzoh meal and salt and pepper to taste and mix thoroughly. Allow the mixture to chill for 2 hours.

4 Bring a large pot of salted water to a boil and then shape the matzoh mixture into walnut-size balls and drop them into a boiling water. Simmer for approximately 30 minutes or until tender. Remove with a slotted spoon and set aside.

5 To serve, reheat the soup until scalding then add the matzoh balls to heat them through. Serve 1–2 matzoh balls per person with a bowl of broth and garnish with extra parsley.

Serves 10 • Preparation 40 minutes • Cooking 6 hours

Lamb

Lamb Shank Soup

30g/2 tablespoons butter
1 large onion, sliced
4 lamb shanks
½ cup barley
3 stalks celery, sliced
2 large carrots, sliced
2 large parsnips, diced
2 tomatoes, diced
1 teaspoon salt
freshly ground black pepper
¼ cup parsley, chopped

1 Melt the butter in a large saucepan. Add the onion and cook over a low heat for 10 minutes. Add the shanks, barley, celery, carrots, parsnips, tomatoes and 12 cups water. Season with salt and pepper. Cover and simmer for 1½–2 hours.

2 Remove the lamb shanks and chop the meat. Return the meat to the soup and discard the bones. Adjust seasoning if necessary.

3 Sprinkle with parsley and serve with crusty bread.

Serves 8 • Preparation 30 minutes • Cooking 2 hours

Lamb and Cheddar Soup

750g/1.65 lb lamb neck bones
1 large onion, finely chopped
3 cloves garlic, finely chopped
2 bay leaves
30g/2 tablespoons butter
2 tablespoons all-purpose flour
1 cup milk
125g/4½ oz Cheddar cheese, grated
4 carrots, diced
2 leeks, finely chopped
3 medium potatoes, peeled and diced
salt and freshly ground black pepper
¼ cup fresh parsley, chopped

1 Place the lamb in a saucepan. Add the onion, garlic and bay leaves and cover with
   4 cups water. Bring to a boil and simmer gently for an hour.
2 Remove the lamb and cut the meat into small pieces – discard the bones, but keep
   the lamb stock.
3 In a large saucepan, melt the butter and add the flour. Cook for a minute, stirring
   all the time, then add the milk.
4 Simmer the sauce for 2 minutes, add the cheese, the lamb stock, lamb pieces and
   vegetables. Simmer gently for 30 minutes, stirring occasionally. Season with salt
   and pepper to taste.
5 Serve garnished with chopped parsley and accompanied with crusty bread.

Serves 4 • Preparation 30 minutes • Cooking 1 hour 10 minutes

Smoky Lamb Stew

1kg/2 lb eggplant
80g/5½ tablespoons butter
2 large leeks
500g/18 oz sweet potato, peeled and cubed
2 teaspoons ground cumin
2 teaspoons ground cinnamon
2kg/4 lb lamb shanks
4 cups beef stock
4 sprigs thyme
3 cinnamon sticks
1 cup flat-leaf parsley, chopped

1 Preheat oven to 425°F/220°C. Prick eggplant all over and roast on an oiled baking sheet until browned and softened, about an hour. Chop the eggplant into bite-size pieces.

2 Heat half the butter in a large saucepan, add the leeks and sauté until golden. Add the chopped eggplant, sweet potato, cumin and ground cinnamon and stir thoroughly while cooking for 5 minutes or until all the ingredients are golden and fragrant. Place this mixture in a bowl and set aside.

3 In the same saucepan, heat the remaining butter and add the lamb shanks, and brown over medium-high heat. Add the beef stock, thyme, cinnamon sticks and 6 cups water and simmer for 1 hour.

4 Remove the shanks and, to the remaining soup, add the eggplant mixture and half the parsley. Simmer for 10 minutes. Cut all the meat off the lamb shanks and return this meat to the soup. Discard the bones.

5 Remove and discard the cinnamon sticks and thyme sprigs, then reheat the soup until simmering. Season to taste with salt and pepper. Add parsley.

Serves 6–8 • Preparation 1 hour • Cooking 2 hours

Lamb Chickpea Stew

1 tablespoon olive oil
1 large brown onion, finely chopped
500g/1 lb lamb stew meat, finely chopped
200g/7 oz canned chickpeas, rinsed and drained
3 tablespoons tomato purée
1 teaspoon ground coriander
1 teaspoon ground turmeric
½ teaspoon chilli powder
½ teaspoon salt
1½ tablespoons dried mint
juice of ½ lemon
6 fresh mint sprigs
1 lemon, cut into wedges

1 Heat the oil in a large casserole or saucepan. Gently fry the onion for a few minutes until pale golden and soft.

2 Add the lamb, chickpeas, tomato purée, spices and salt, cooking for a few more minutes and stirring well.

3 Add 4 cups water to the saucepan – this should cover the mixture – then add 1 cup more if required. If adding extra water, remember that you may need to add a little extra spice and salt to compensate.

4 Cover and simmer over a medium heat for approx 45–50 minutes or until the lamb is tender. If required, you may add a little extra water again at this point, but remember to adjust the seasoning if you do.

5 Add the dried mint and the lemon juice, return to the heat for an additional 3–4 minutes then serve each bowl with a sprig of fresh mint and a lemon wedge on the side.

Serves 6 • Preparation 20 minutes • Cooking 1 hour

Pork

Broccoli Soup with Bacon

1 tablespoon olive oil
1 large onion, roughly chopped
2 cloves garlic, chopped
3 cups chicken stock
500g/1 lb broccoli
3 slices bacon, cooked and crumbled
1 cup milk
freshly ground black pepper

1 Heat the oil in a large saucepan and sauté the onion and garlic for 5 minutes until clear. Pour in stock and bring to a boil.
2 Add broccoli and cook for 10 minutes until just tender. Purée in a blender or food processor.
3 Return soup to saucepan. Mix in bacon and milk. Cook for 5 minutes. Season with freshly ground black pepper. Serve garnished with chopped chives.

Serves 4 • Preparation 15 minutes • Cooking 30 minutes

Corn and Bacon Chowder

6 slices bacon, chopped
1 medium onion, thinly sliced
500g/1 lb potatoes, peeled and medium diced
880g/28 oz canned creamed corn
3 cups milk
1 sprig thyme, leaves removed and stalk discarded
salt and freshly ground black pepper
dash of Worcestershire sauce

1 Place bacon in a saucepan and sautè over medium heat until crisp. Remove and drain on absorbent paper.
2 Sautè onion until tender, add potatoes and 5 cups boiling water and cook for an additional 10 minutes. Add sweetcorn, milk, thyme and bacon, bring to a boil, season with salt, pepper and Worcestershire sauce. Garnish with extra fresh thyme or parsley.

Serves 8 • Preparation 30 minutes • Cooking 30 minutes

Egg Drop Soup

4 cups chicken stock
1½ tablespoons soy sauce
1 teaspoon sugar
2 eggs, lightly beaten
1 slice of ham, finely diced
2 green onions, finely chopped

1 Bring stock to a boil, and add soy sauce and sugar.
2 Just before serving, pour the eggs into the hot stock, but do not stir. As soon as the eggs start to cook, stir gently. Garnish with ham and green onions and serve immediately.

Serves 4 • Preparation 15 minutes • Cooking 15 minutes

Split Pea Soup

250g/9 oz dried split peas
500g/1 lb ham hocks or ham bones
2 carrots, roughly chopped
2 turnips, roughly chopped
2 onions, roughly chopped
4 stalks celery, chopped
salt and freshly ground black pepper
1 tablespoon all-purpose flour, mixed with 1 tablespoon water

1 Wash peas and soak in water overnight. Place peas, water and bones in a saucepan and bring to a boil. Add prepared vegetables and simmer for 1½ hours.
2 Remove bones, purée mixture, and season with salt and pepper. Thicken with flour paste and, stirring continuously, cook for 3 minutes. Garnish with croutons and serve immediately.

Serves 8 • Preparation 30 minutes • Cooking 2 hours

Pork and Vegetable Soup

400g/14 oz boneless pork, cut into ½ in/15mm cubes
2 tablespoons all-purpose flour
1 tablespoon vegetable oil
1 medium onion, chopped
2 stalks celery, diced
3 cups chicken stock
½ teaspoon dried marjoram
2 medium potatoes, peeled and diced
125g/4½ oz mushrooms, chopped
½ medium green bell pepper, chopped
2 tablespoons diced pimiento
¼ cup flat-leaf parsley, chopped

1 Place pork and flour in a plastic bag and shake until coated.

2 Heat oil in a large saucepan. Add the pork and brown lightly.

3 Add onion and sauté 2–3 minutes longer. Add celery, stock and marjoram. Bring to a boil. Cover and simmer for 15 minutes.

4 Add potatoes and mushrooms. Bring to a boil again. Cover and simmer for 10 minutes. Stir in green pepper and pimiento. Simmer for 5 minutes more.

5 Sprinkle with parsley. Ladle into bowls.

Serves 4 • Preparation 20 minutes • Cooking 45 minutes

Southwestern Pork Stew

1 tablespoon olive oil
1 medium onion, chopped
½ green bell pepper, chopped
4 large cloves garlic, minced
1 jalapeño pepper, seeded and minced
500g/1 lb pork tenderloin, trimmed and cut into bite-size pieces
2 cups chicken stock
2 teaspoons chilli powder
1 teaspoon ground cumin
½ teaspoon salt
¼ teaspoon black pepper
500g/18 oz canned pinto beans, rinsed and drained
400g/14 oz canned diced tomatoes, undrained
¼ cup fresh cilantro, chopped
1 avocado, diced

1 Heat a small non-stick casserole dish over medium-heat and add oil.

2 Add onion, bell pepper, garlic and jalapeño and sauté for 2 minutes.

3 Add pork and cook for 3 minutes. Add stock, chilli powder, cumin, salt, pepper, pinto beans and tomatoes and bring to a boil.

4 Partially cover, reduce heat, and simmer for 6 minutes or until pork is done, stirring occasionally. Remove from heat and stir in cilantro. Serve with avocado.

Serves 4 • Preparation 20 minutes • Cooking 15 minutes

Stone Soup

1 tablespoon olive oil
1 onion, finely chopped
2 cloves garlic, crushed
200g/7 oz smoked bacon, diced
250g/9 oz smoked ham hock
2 potatoes, diced
2 carrots, diced
2 turnips, diced
2 stalks celery, diced
2 bay leaves
6 cups vegetable or chicken stock
150g/5 oz Savoy or green cabbage, shredded
400g/14 oz canned red kidney beans, drained and rinsed
¼ cup fresh parsley, chopped
salt and freshly ground black pepper

1 Heat the oil in a large saucepan over medium heat. Cook the onion and garlic until soft. Add the bacon and cook for 2 minutes. Add the ham hock, potatoes, carrots, turnips, celery, bay leaves and stock.

2 Bring to a boil, reduce heat to low and simmer covered for 40–45 minutes or until vegetables are tender. If time permits, simmer for 1 hour, as this gives the soup more flavor. Add cabbage and kidney beans and simmer for an additional 5 minutes.

3 Remove ham hock and cut the meat into small pieces. Return meat to the saucepan, add parsley and season with salt and pepper. Serve with crusty bread.

Serves 4–6 • Preparation 25 minutes • Cooking 2 hours

Seafood

Clam Chowder

45g/3 tablespoons butter
3 rashers bacon, chopped
1 onion, chopped
1 stalk celery, chopped
1 carrot, chopped
1 potato, peeled and chopped
280g/9–10 oz canned clams, drained and chopped
3 tablespoons all-purpose flour
2½ cups milk
salt and freshly ground black pepper
1 tablespoon brandy

1 Melt 1 tablespoon of butter in pan, add bacon and vegetables and cook gently until soft.
2 Add 1¼ cups water and potatoes to vegetables. Simmer until vegetables are tender, approximately 15–20 minutes.
3 Add clams to vegetables and remove the pan from the heat.
4 Melt remaining butter in pan, stir in the flour and cook for 1 minute. Remove from heat and gradually stir in milk.
5 Return soup to heat and add milk mixture. Cook until soup boils and thickens, stirring constantly. Season with salt and pepper, stir in the brandy and serve.

Serves 6 • Preparation 20 minutes • Cooking 30 minutes

Fish Stew

60g/4 tablespoons butter
1 small leek, washed and thinly sliced
1 medium carrot, thinly sliced
1 small onion, chopped
1 tablespoon curry powder
1 tomato, peeled, seeded and chopped
2 cups fish stock
1 large potato, peeled and diced
1 teaspoon brown sugar
½ teaspoon salt
250g/9 oz fish filets, cut into 1 in/25mm pieces
salt and freshly ground black pepper
1 cup heavy cream
¼ cup parsley, chopped

1 Heat butter in a saucepan and sauté leek, carrot and onion over a low heat for
   5 minutes or until the vegetables are tender.
2 Stir in curry powder and cook for 2 minutes. Add tomato and cook for 5 minutes.
   Stir in stock, potato, sugar and salt and bring to a boil. Reduce the heat and
   simmer for 15 minutes.
3 Add fish and seasonings and simmer for an additional 10 minutes. Stir through
   cream and reheat without boiling. Sprinkle with parsley and serve.

Serves 8 • Preparation 30 minutes • Cooking 45 minutes

Crab Corn Chowder

1 cup white wine
2 cloves garlic, crushed
4 cups good fish stock
1 teaspoon dried oregano
3 green onions, sliced
220g/8 oz can crab meat, drained
400g/14 oz can creamed corn
¾ cup heavy cream
2 egg yolks
12 oysters
2 tablespoons fresh chopped basil
salt and freshly ground black pepper

1 Heat wine in a large saucepan over medium heat. Add garlic and simmer for 2–3 minutes.

2 Add fish stock, oregano, green onions, crab, corn and half the cream. Bring to a boil, reduce heat to low. Cover and simmer for 5 minutes.

3 Combine remaining cream with egg yolks. Gently stir cream and eggs into soup. Do not allow soup to boil.

4 Remove from heat stir through oysters and basil and season with salt and pepper.

Serves 4 • Preparation 20 minutes • Cooking 15 minutes

Creamy Mussel Soup

1kg/2 lb fresh mussels
500g/1 lb shrimp with shells on
1 large onion, chopped
2 stalks celery, chopped
2 large carrots, chopped
¼ cup parsley, chopped
8 cups fish stock
2 cups white wine
3 shallots, chopped
1¼ cups heavy cream
salt and freshly ground black pepper

1 Scrub and remove beards from mussels. Soak in clean water for at least 3 hours before use. Peel shrimp, place the heads and shells into a boiling pot. Reserve the peeled shrimp for another meal or deep freeze for another occasion.

2 Add the onion, celery, carrot, parsley, fish stock and white wine to the pot. Bring to a boil and then simmer for 45 minutes. Strain and reserve stock.

3 Place the mussels in a suitable size pot, pour in the stock and add the shallots. Boil for 20 minutes. If you need more liquid, add some white wine. Before serving, add the cream and check seasoning. Serve with fresh crusty bread.

Serves 6 • Preparation 1 hour • Cooking 1 hour 10 minutes

Shrimp and Pasta Soup

1½kg/3 lb cooked shrimp
1 small onion, chopped
1 stalk celery, chopped
1 small carrot, chopped
300g/10 oz cooked pasta
2 tablespoons olive oil
4 large cloves garlic, chopped
4 sprigs fresh oregano, leaves removed and chopped
1 large sprig basil, chopped
400g/14 oz canned chopped tomatoes
2 tablespoons tomato paste
1 teaspoon salt
1 teaspoon freshly ground black pepper
½ cup dry vermouth

1 Peel the shrimp, place the heads and shells into a boiling pot, add the onion, celery and carrot. Cover with 6 cups water and boil for 20 minutes, then strain. Reserve the stock and make sure you push all the juice from the heads with the back of a wooden spoon. Discard the solids.

2 Bring a large saucepan of salted water to a boil, add the pasta and cook for 8 minutes or until just firm in the center (al dente). Drain, set aside and keep warm.

3 In a saucepan, heat the oil, add all remaining ingredients except the shrimp and cook for 5 minutes. Add the stock and boil for an additional 15 minutes. Reduce the heat, add the shrimp and cook for 3 minutes.

4 Reheat the pasta by pan frying or running under hot water. Divide between six soup bowls and ladle the soup into the bowls. Serve with crusty bread.

Serves 6 • Preparation 40 minutes • Cooking 1 hour

Seafood Bisque

90g/6 tablespoons butter
1 small onion, diced
1 clove garlic, crushed
1 small carrot, diced
1 stalk celery, sliced
3 cups fish stock
2 tablespoons lemon juice
1 bay leaf
1 sprig thyme, leaves removed and stalks discarded
¼ teaspoon Tabasco sauce
½ teaspoon Worcestershire sauce
1 cup heavy cream
1kg/2 lb seafood (shrimp, scallops, fresh fish filets), finely diced
½ cup dry white wine
1 lemon, thinly sliced
¼ cup parsley, chopped

1 Melt butter and sauté onion and garlic for 5 minutes. Add carrot and celery and cook for an additional 3 minutes.
2 Combine the fish stock, lemon juice, bay leaf, thyme, Tabasco and Worcestershire sauce, add to the pot and simmer for 30 minutes or until vegetables are tender. Remove bay leaf. Puree the mixture, add cream, seafood, wine, and reheat, but do not let boil. Garnish with lemon and parsley.

Serves 8 • Preparation 40 minutes • Cooking 45 minutes

Spicy Thai Soup

1 tablespoon vegetable oil
550g/1 lb raw shrimp, shells removed and reserved
2 small red chilies, seeded and cut into long thin strips
1 tablespoon paprika
¼ teaspoon ground red pepper
1½ quarts/liters chicken stock
¾ in/2cm strip lemon zest
¾ in/2cm strip lime zest
1 can straw mushrooms, drained
juice of 1 lemon
juice of ½ lime
2 tablespoons light soy sauce
fresh cilantro, to garnish

1 Heat wok over medium-high heat for 2 minutes. Add oil to wok: it should start to smoke. Carefully add shrimp and 1 red chilli and stir-fry for 1 minute.

2 Add paprika and ground red pepper. Stir-fry for 1 minute longer. Remove shrimp mixture and set aside.

3 Add shrimp shells to wok and stir-fry for 2 minutes until shells turn orange. Add chicken stock and lemon and lime zest and bring to a boil. Cover, reduce heat and simmer for 15 minutes. Strain the soup and return the liquid to the saucepan.

4 Add mushrooms and shrimp mixture to the soup and bring to a simmer. Stir in the lemon and lime juice, soy sauce and remaining red chilli. Garnish with fresh cilantro.

Serves 4 • Preparation 10 minutes • Cooking 25 minutes

Vegetable

Provençal-Style Soup

2 tablespoons extra virgin olive oil
1 onion, chopped
1 medium potato, peeled and chopped
1 carrot, chopped
1 yellow bell pepper, deseeded and chopped
500mL/17 oz vegetable stock
2 stalks celery, chopped
2 zucchini, chopped
400g/14 oz canned chopped tomatoes
1 tablespoon tomato purée
sea salt and freshly ground black pepper

Green onion Pesto
6 green onions, roughly chopped
50g/1.8 oz Parmesan, grated
4 tablespoons extra virgin olive oil

1 For the soup, heat the oil in a large heavy-based saucepan, then add the onion,
   potato, carrot and yellow bell pepper. Cook uncovered for 5 minutes over a
   medium heat, stirring occasionally, until the vegetables just start to brown.

2 Add the stock, celery and zucchini and bring to a boil. Cover and simmer for
   10 minutes or until the vegetables are tender. Stir in the tomatoes, tomato purée
   and season generously. Simmer uncovered for 10 minutes.

3 Meanwhile, make the pesto. Place the green onions, Parmesan and oil in a food
   processor and process together to a fairly smooth paste. Ladle the soup into
   bowls and top with a spoonful of the pesto.

Serves 4–6 • Preparation 20 minutes • Cooking 25 minutes

Cauliflower Soup

750g/1½ lb cauliflower florets
200g/7 oz onions, chopped
6 cups chicken stock
6 cups milk
2 teaspoons salt
¼ teaspoon cayenne pepper
½ cup heavy cream
¼ cup parsley, chopped

1 Combine the cauliflower, onions, stock and milk in a large boiling pot. Cook until the cauliflower is broken down. Remove from heat.

2 Blend the cauliflower and liquid, then return to the pot.

3 Season with salt and cayenne pepper, then add the cream. Reheat and serve garnished with chopped parsley.

Serves 8 • Preparation 30 minutes • Cooking 40 minutes

Tomato Leek Soup

400g/14 oz white leek, washed and finely chopped
6 cups chicken stock
600g/20 oz tomatoes, peeled, seeded and chopped
1 teaspoon salt
½ teaspoon lemon pepper
1 sprig basil, chopped

1 Place the finely chopped leeks into a boiling pot and cover with the chicken stock. Bring to a boil. Cook for an additional 5 minutes and then add the tomato. Boil until the tomato is cooked. Remove from the heat and add the salt, lemon pepper and basil. Serve with a spoonful of sour cream and a sprig of basil.

Serves 6 • Preparation 30 minutes • Cooking 45 minutes

Chunky Tomato Soup

750g/1½ lb ripe tomatoes, chopped
1 potato, peeled and chopped
1 small onion, chopped
1 sprig fresh basil
1 teaspoon sugar
2 tablespoons tomato paste
salt and freshly ground black pepper
1 cup vegetable stock
¼ cup heavy cream
¼ cup parsley, finely chopped

1 Place all ingredients except parsley and cream into a saucepan with the stock. Bring to a boil and simmer, covered, for 20 minutes.

2 Serve soup with a swirl of cream and sprinkle with chopped parsley.

Serves 4 • Preparation 20 minutes • Cooking 30 minutes

Cream of Asparagus Soup

1kg/2 lb fresh asparagus
2 tablespoons butter
4 large shallots, finely chopped
20 basil leaves
6 tablespoons flour
pinch of saffron threads

6 cups chicken or vegetable stock
salt and freshly ground pepper to taste
2 egg yolks
1 cup whole milk or half and half
peanut oil for frying
large basil leaves, extra

1 Cut the tips off the asparagus and drop in boiling water for 30 seconds. Drain and set aside. Cut the remaining stalks into ¾ in/2cm lengths. Melt the butter and sauté the asparagus stalks for two minutes. Add the shallots and basil leaves and continue cooking for 5 minutes or until the vegetables have softened.

2 Sprinkle the flour over the vegetable mixture and stir thoroughly, making sure that all the flour is mixed in. Add the saffron and chicken or vegetable stock and bring the mixture to a boil, stirring often.

3 Simmer for 20 minutes or until the vegetables are tender. Puree the soup with a blender or food processor. Return to saucepan and season with salt and pepper.

4 Whisk the egg yolks and milk together. Slowly add to the puréed soup, whisking constantly. Cook over low heat for five minutes, until hot.

5 To prepare the fried basil leaves, heat a little peanut oil then add a few basil leaves at a time (take care as leaves will splatter for a few seconds). Remove the leaves as soon as they stop sizzling and drain on paper towel. Repeat with remaining basil leaves. Garnish with the reserved asparagus tips, fried basil leaves, and a drizzle of cream.

This rich soup, with a subtle flavor of saffron and basil is delicious hot or at room temperature.

Serves 6–8 • Preparation 30 minutes • Cooking 40 minutes

Vegetable Soup with Pesto

500g/18 oz cannellini beans, rinsed and drained
1 large onion
500g/18 oz green beans
500g/18 oz zucchini
5 medium potatoes
30g/2 tablespoons butter
2–3 slices bacon, chopped
8–10 cups water
2 teaspoons salt

Tomato Basil Paste
1 cup basil leaves, finely shredded
4 cloves garlic, crushed
2 ripe tomatoes, peeled and chopped
1 tablespoon tomato paste
½ cup romano cheese, grated
3 tablespoons olive oil

1 Chop the onion finely. Trim the green beans and cut into short lengths. Cut zucchini into thick slices. Peel the potatoes and dice.

2 Melt butter in a large pan and sauté bacon and prepared vegetables until softened, about 5 minutes. Add cannellini beans and salt; cover with cold water, cover and simmer gently for 1 hour.

3 Combine basil leaves and garlic in a food processor. Add tomatoes, tomato paste and cheese. Puree. Gradually pour in olive oil and puree until smooth. Stir into the soup just before serving.

Tomato Basil Paste

1 Combine basil leaves and garlic in a bowl. Add the tomatoes to the basil with tomato paste and cheese. Pound this mixture in a blender or food processor to make a smooth paste. Gradually beat in olive oil. Set aside to serve with soup.

Serves 4–6 • Preparation 10 minutes plus soaking • Cooking 1 hour 30 minutes

Roasted Tomato, Red Pepper and Bread Soup

1kg/2 lb plum tomatoes
2 red peppers
3 tablespoons extra-virgin olive oil
3 cloves garlic, crushed
2 onions, finely chopped
2 teaspoons ground cumin
1 teaspoon turmeric
1 teaspoon ground cilantro
4 cups vegetable or chicken stock
2 slices whole-wheat bread, crusts removed and torn into pieces
1 tablespoon balsamic vinegar
salt and pepper

1 Preheat the oven to 425°F/220°C.
2 Place the tomatoes and peppers in a lightly oiled baking dish and bake for 20 minutes or until the skins have blistered. Set aside to cool, then remove the skins and roughly chop.
3 Heat the oil in a saucepan, add the garlic and onion and cook for 5 minutes, or until soft. Add the cumin, turmeric and cilantro, and cook for 1 minute until well combined. Add tomatoes, peppers and bouillon to the saucepan, bring to a boil and simmer for 30 minutes. Add bread, balsamic vinegar and salt and pepper, and cook for an additional 5–10 minutes.
4 Serve with fresh cilantro and Parmesan cheese, if desired.

Serves 4 • Preparation 10 minutes • Cooking 1 hour

Butternut Squash Soup

1 tablespoon olive oil
1 onion, finely chopped
2 cloves garlic, crushed
1 long red chilli, deseeded and finely chopped
5 cups vegetable or chicken stock
1kg butternut pumpkin, peeled and diced
2 tomatoes, roughly chopped
½ cup cream
2 tablespoons freshly chopped cilantro
1 tablespoons freshly chopped mint
salt and freshly ground black pepper
¼ cup grated Parmesan cheese

1 Heat oil in a large saucepan over medium heat. Cook onion, garlic and chilies until soft.
2 Add stock, pumpkin and tomatoes. Bring to a boil, reduce heat to low. Cover and simmer for 20 minutes or until pumpkin is tender.
3 Puree soup until smooth. Return soup to the heat. Stir through cream, cilantro and mint. Season with salt and pepper.
4 Serve soup with grated parmesan cheese.

Serves 4–6 • Preparation 20 minutes • Cooking 30 minutes

Spicy Sweet Potato Soup

1 tablespoon olive oil
1 leek, halved, washed and sliced
3 cloves garlic, freshly crushed
1½ tablespoons Thai seasoning
750g/1½ lb sweet potatoes, peeled and roughly chopped
750g/1½ lb carrots, peeled and roughly chopped
5 cups chicken stock
400mL/14 oz coconut milk or light coconut milk
salt and freshly ground black pepper

1 Heat the oil in a large saucepan. Over medium heat add the leek and garlic and cook until soft. Add the Thai seasoning and cook until aromatic.

2 Add the sweet potatoes, carrots, stock and coconut milk. Bring to a boil. Cover and simmer for 30 minutes or until the vegetables are soft.

3 Purée the soup in a blender until smooth. Return the soup to the saucepan and cook until heated. Season to taste. Spoon into bowls and drizzle with extra coconut milk. Serve with crusty bread.

Cut off and discard the root and green leaves from the leek. Cut the white part of the leek in half lengthways. Remove the outer layer and wash the leaves to remove the dirt.

Serves 4–6 • Preparation 15 minutes • Cooking 33 minutes

Mushroom Barley Soup

4 tablespoons butter or oil
1 large onion, finely diced
2 quarts/liters beef stock
1 medium carrot, peeled and diced
1 large potato, peeled and diced
½ cup pearl barley
1 bay leaf
1 tablespoon chopped fresh dill or ½ teaspoon dried
500g/18 oz button or field mushrooms
1½ tablespoons lemon juice
thin cut lemon slices for garnish

1 Heat half the butter or oil in a large saucepan, add the onion and gently fry until soft. Stir in the stock and bring to a boil. Add the carrot, potato, barley, bay leaf and dill. Simmer for 1 hour, stirring occasionally.

2 Wipe over the mushrooms with damp paper, trim the stem end and slice mushroom thinly.

3 In a large pan heat remaining butter or oil and fry the mushrooms gently for 3–5 minutes tossing frequently. Add to the simmering soup and simmer for 15–20 minutes more. Taste and adjust seasoning and stir in the lemon juice.

4 Serve in soup bowls garnished with lemon slices and sprig of dill floating on surface.

Serves 6–8 • Preparation 25 minutes • Cooking 1 hour 30 minutes

Pumpkin Soup

1½kg/3 lb pumpkin, peeled and cut into large cubes
2 tomatoes, chopped
1 large onion, chopped
5 cups vegetable stock
pinch of salt
pinch of cayenne pepper
⅔ cup heavy cream
¼ cup parsley, finely chopped

1 Combine pumpkin, tomato and onions with the stock in a pan. Simmer gently until pumpkin is tender, approximately 20 minutes.
2 Purée pumpkin mixture. Return to pan, add salt, cayenne pepper and cream and reheat gently.
3 Serve sprinkled with parsley.

Pumpkin soup is also delicious chilled

Serves 6 • Preparation 20 minutes • Cooking 30 minutes

Minestrone

⅓ cup olive oil
1 medium onion, sliced
1 clove garlic, crushed
250g/½ lb potatoes, peeled and chopped
150g/5 oz carrots, thinly sliced
125g/4½ oz celery, thinly sliced
150g/5 oz zucchini, sliced
4 cups vegetable stock
400g/14 oz canned diced tomatoes
rind from piece of Parmesan cheese
¼ cup parsley, chopped
400g/14 oz canned cannellini beans
salt and freshly ground black pepper

1 Heat the oil in a saucepan and cook the onion and garlic for 5 minutes until onion
   is tender. Add the potatoes and cook for an additional 5 minutes. Repeat with the
   carrots, celery and zucchini.
2 Add the beef stock, tomatoes and cheese rind, bring to a boil and simmer covered for
   1 hour. If the soup becomes too thick, add more stock.
3 Add the chopped parsley and cannellini beans, and heat for an additional 10 minutes.
4 To serve, remove the cheese rind, season with salt and black pepper, and serve with
   crusty bread.

Serves 6 • Preparation 20 minutes • Cooking 1 hour 30 minutes

Roasted Vegetable Soup

2 tablespoons extra virgin olive oil
1 large sweet onion, chopped
2 carrots, peeled and diced
2 stalks celery, chopped
2 cloves garlic, minced
½ in/1cm piece fresh ginger, finely chopped
3 teaspoons fennel seeds, dry-fried for 2 minutes then crushed
½ fennel bulb, chopped
1 teaspoon sea salt
800g/28 oz canned crushed tomatoes
3 cups vegetable stock
freshly ground black pepper
¼ cup fresh cilantro, chopped

1 Heat oil in heavy saucepan. Add onion and sauté on medium heat until translucent.

2 Add carrots, celery, garlic, fresh ginger, crushed fennel seeds, fresh fennel bulb and sea salt. Simmer until soft, approximately 5–10 minutes.

3 Add tomatoes, stir and cook briefly. Add vegetable stock. Bring to a boil, stirring constantly. Cover and simmer for 20 minutes.

4 Place small amounts in a blender or food processor and blend until smooth. Return to saucepan. Add fresh ground pepper, and cilantro. Stir and serve, garnished with chopped fennel leaves.

Serves 4 • Preparation 10 minutes • Cooking 30 minutes

Potato Watercress Soup

1 medium bunch watercress, coarsely chopped
1kg/2 lb potatoes, peeled and roughly chopped
4 cups milk
1¼ cups vegetable stock
salt and freshly ground black pepper
chopped fennel leaves

1 Simmer the potatoes in the milk and stock. Add the watercress when the potatoes are nearly cooked, then cook for an additional 10 minutes.
2 Purée the ingredients in a blender or food processor. Season with salt and pepper, and chill completely. Serve with the chopped fennel or dill leaves. Garnish with croutons and sour cream.

Serves 4 • Preparation 25 minutes • Cooking 50 minutes

Corn and Red Pepper Chowder

1 sprig fresh cilantro
30g/2 tablespoons butter
400g/14 oz canned corn
2 red bell peppers, diced
1 small onion, finely chopped
1 small red chili, finely chopped
1 tablespoon all-purpose flour
2 cups vegetable stock
½ cup heavy cream

1 Trim the leaves off the fresh cilantro and finely chop the root and stems.
2 Heat the butter in a large saucepan over medium heat. Add the corn kernels, bell pepper, onion and chilli and stir to coat the vegetables in the butter. Cook, covered, over low heat, stirring occasionally, for 10 minutes, or until the vegetables are soft.
3 Increase the heat to medium and add the cilantro root and stem. Cook, stirring, for 30 seconds, or until fragrant. Sprinkle with the flour and stir for an additional minute.
4 Remove from the heat and gradually add the vegetable stock, stirring together.
5 Add 2 cups water and return to the heat. Bring to a boil, reduce the heat to low and simmer, covered, for 30 minutes, or until the vegetables are tender. Cool slightly.
6 Ladle about 2 cups of the soup into a blender and purée until smooth. Return the purée to the soup in the saucepan, pour in the cream and gently heat until warmed through. Season to taste with salt. Sprinkle with the cilantro leaves to serve.

Serves 2 • Preparation 35 minutes • Cooking 1 hour

Cold

Red Pepper Fennel Soup

2 tablespoons olive oil
2 leeks, white part only, chopped
1 onion, chopped
2 cloves garlic, chopped
2 shallots, chopped
5 large carrots, chopped
2 fennel bulbs, halved, cored and chopped
4 sprigs fresh thyme
2–3 red bell peppers
1 cup white wine
4½ cups chicken or vegetable stock
salt and freshly ground pepper
3 tablespoons plain yogurt

Corn Mint Salsa
2 ears of corn
½ small onion, finely diced
1 Roma or plum tomato, seeded
10 fresh mint leaves, finely sliced
2 sprigs fresh cilantro, chopped
⅓ cup chopped fresh parsley
juice of 1 lime
salt and freshly ground pepper

1 Heat the olive oil in a saucepan and add the leeks, onion, garlic and shallots and sweat for 5 minutes until soft. Add the carrots, fennel and thyme sprigs and cook over a medium heat for 30 minutes until all the vegetables are tender.

2 Grill the red peppers until blackened and blistered. Transfer to a plastic bag and allow to steam for a few minutes. When cool enough to handle, remove the skins and slice the peppers into strips.

3 Add peppers, wine and stock to the softened vegetables, and cook, uncovered on high heat for about 20 minutes. Remove from heat and puree in a food processor or blender. Season to taste with salt and pepper and chill for 1 hour.

4 Make salsa by cutting the corn off the ears and microwaving for 2 minutes. Stir in the onion, tomato, herbs and lime juice. Season to taste.

Serves 8 • Preparation 25 minutes plus 1 hour chilling • Cooking 1 hour 5 minutes

Gazpacho

2 slices of stale bread
2kg/4 lb tomatoes, roughly chopped
1 cucumber, peeled and chopped
1 green bell pepper, seeded and chopped
1 small onion, chopped
2 cloves garlic, chopped
5 tablespoons olive oil
1–2 tablespoons wine vinegar
1 teaspoon cumin seeds or ground cumin

1 Soak bread in a little water, and squeeze it out before using (the bread helps to thicken the soup and give it a nice consistency).

2 Blend all vegetables and garlic in a blender or food processor, and push through a strainer into a bowl. Use the blender again to mix bread, oil and vinegar together. Add some of the tomatoes, the cumin seeds and salt to taste. Add a little water and mix into the bowl with the soup. Add a few ice cubes and let sit until chilled, adding more water if necessary.

Serves 6–8 • Preparation 15 minutes plus 2 hours chilling

Iced Tomato Soup

3 slices bread, crusts removed
1kg/2 lb tomatoes, peeled, seeded and chopped
1 cucumber, peeled, deseeded and chopped
½ onion, chopped
2 cloves garlic, crushed
½ green bell pepper, deseeded and chopped
1 teaspoon salt
1 teaspoon ground cumin
2 tablespoons olive oil
2 tablespoons wine vinegar

Garnish
1 red or green bell pepper, diced
1 small cucumber, diced
1 onion, finely chopped
2 hard-boiled eggs, chopped
croutons

1 Place all ingredients in a large bowl and allow to stand for 30 minutes to soften bread and blend flavors.

2 Purée one-third of the mixture at a time in a blender or food processor. Pour back into a bowl and thin down to desired consistency with 2–3 cups iced water.

3 Cover and chill. Adjust seasoning to taste. Serve in chilled bowls or in a large bowl over ice.

4 Garnish with assorted toppings.

Serves 8 • Preparation 20 minutes plus 2 hours chilling

Cool Cumin-Yogurt Soup

1 teaspoon cumin seeds
1 teaspoon black cumin seeds
1 tablespoon butter
4 green onions, finely sliced
10 fresh mint leaves
2 teaspoons ground cumin
1 teaspoon turmeric
60g/¼ cup cashews
300g/10 oz can chickpeas, drained and rinsed

500g/18 oz plain lowfat yogurt
200mL/8 oz sour cream
200mL/8 oz water
salt and pepper to taste
600g/1⅓ lb cucumbers
1 tablespoon sugar
2 tablespoons shredded coconut, toasted
mint leaves, for garnish

1 Heat a dry skillet. Add cumin seeds and toss until toasted, about 3 minutes. Remove from the pan and set aside.

2 Add the butter to the pan and add green onions and mint leaves and sauté for a few minutes until wilted. Add the cumin, turmeric and cashews and toss until the spices are fragrant and the nuts are golden. Add the drained chickpeas and cook for an additional 2 minutes. Set aside.

3 In a mixing bowl, whisk together the yogurt, sour cream and water until smooth. Season to taste with salt and pepper. Peel the cucumbers and scrape out the seeds. Cut the cucumber flesh into thin slices and add to the yogurt mixture. Chill for 1 hour before serving.

4 Add the green onion/spice mixture and sugar to the yogurt and stir thoroughly to combine.

5 Garnish with toasted coconut, sliced mint leaves and cumin seeds.

Serves 6 • Preparation 30 minutes • Cooking 1 hour 15 minutes

Vichyssoise

60g/4 tablespoons butter
2 leeks, washed and thinly sliced
1 medium onion, thinly sliced
500g/18 oz potatoes, peeled and sliced
3 cups chicken stock
salt and freshly ground black pepper
¾ cup heavy cream
¼ small bunch chives, chopped

1 Melt butter in a saucepan, add leeks and onion and sauté until tender without browning. Add potatoes, stock and seasonings and simmer until soft. Purée.
2 Chill for 2–3 hours. Adjust seasonings, stir in the cream and serve in chilled bowls garnished with chopped chives.

Serves 4 • Preparation 20 minutes plus 2–3 hours chilling • Cooking 40 minutes

Cantaloupe Soup

1 large cantaloupe, halved and seeds removed
4 tablespoons/60g butter
2 teaspoons sugar
grated zest of 1 lemon
pinch of salt
3 cups milk
sprigs of mint

1 Using a melon baller, scoop out 12 balls of melon and reserve. Coarsely chop the remaining flesh.
2 Heat the butter over a low heat, add the coarsely chopped melon, sugar, lemon zest and salt and simmer for 4 minutes. Add milk and bring to a boil.
3 Purée mixture and chill. Garnish with reserved melon balls and mint sprigs.

Serves 4 • Preparation 15 minutes plus 2–3 hours chilling • Cooking 15 minutes

Index